TOP FRANKFURT TRAVEL GUIDE

Explore with Ease and Comfort | Attractions, Tips, Maps, and More!"

Oliva. A Raymond

Rights Reserved.

TABLE OF CONTENTS

Welcome to Frankfurt

Paul had always been intrigued by the blend of modernity and history that cities like Frankfurt offered. As an avid traveler, he had explored many destinations, but Frankfurt's reputation as a dynamic financial hub and a cultural melting pot had captured his imagination. With his backpack and camera in tow, he set off to experience all that Frankfurt had to offer.

Upon arriving at Frankfurt Airport, Paul was immediately struck by the city's cosmopolitan atmosphere. The sleek architecture and bustling terminals mirrored the city's reputation as a global business center. Eager to explore, he hopped on a train and made his way to the heart of the city.

Paul had chosen a hotel in the Altstadt, the historic old town of Frankfurt. Wandering through its charming streets, he marveled at the blend of medieval and modern architecture. He couldn't resist stepping into St. Bartholomew's Cathedral, where he gazed in awe at the intricate details of its Gothic design.

With a map in hand, Paul set off to explore some of Frankfurt's iconic landmarks. He made his way to the Römer, the historic town hall square, where the half-timbered buildings seemed to whisper stories of centuries gone by. He paused to take photos and imagine the bustling markets and celebrations that had taken place there over the years.

As a lover of literature, Paul was excited to visit the birthplace of Johann Wolfgang von Goethe, one of Germany's most celebrated writers. The Goethe House offered a glimpse into the life of this literary giant, and Paul found himself inspired by the artifacts and stories that surrounded him.

But Frankfurt wasn't just about history; it was also a city of innovation. Paul explored the modern skyscrapers that dominated the skyline, including the famous Commerzbank Tower. He even ventured to the Main Tower, where he ascended to the observation deck to enjoy panoramic views of the city and the meandering River Main.

The city's vibrant culinary scene didn't disappoint either. Paul indulged in traditional German dishes like schnitzel and bratwurst, and he couldn't resist trying the local apple wine. He discovered cozy cafes tucked away in narrow alleys, where he savored rich coffees and delicious pastries.

One of the highlights of his visit was a stroll along the Museumsufer, the museum embankment that housed a diverse range of museums and galleries. Paul spent hours exploring the Städel Museum, the Museum of Modern Art, and the German Film Museum. Each exhibit offered a unique perspective on art, culture, and history.

Paul also found time to connect with the locals. He struck up conversations with shopkeepers, chatted with fellow travelers in cafes, and joined a walking tour led by a passionate local guide. Through these interactions, he gained insights into the city's daily life, its people, and their perspectives on its evolution.

As his time in Frankfurt drew to a close, Paul felt a sense of gratitude for the experiences he had encountered. The juxtaposition of old and new, the rich history, and the vibrant culture had left an indelible mark on him.

With a heart full of memories and a camera filled with snapshots of the city's beauty, Paul boarded his flight back home. He knew that Frankfurt's unique blend of tradition and modernity would forever remain a cherished chapter in his travel journey. And as he looked out of the plane window, he made a silent promise to return one day, eager to uncover even more of Frankfurt's hidden treasures.

CHAPTER 1: INTRODUCTION

Overview of the City

Frankfurt, often referred to as "Mainhattan" due to its stunning skyline resembling Manhattan's, is a vibrant metropolis located in the heart of Germany. Nestled on the banks of the River Main, Frankfurt is a city where history and modernity seamlessly blend, creating a unique atmosphere that caters to both business and leisure travelers.

Historic Significance
Frankfurt boasts a rich history that dates back to Roman times. It served as a vital trading hub during the Middle Ages and later gained prominence as the site of the

coronation of emperors in the Holy Roman Empire. The iconic Romer Square, with its distinctive medieval buildings, stands as a testament to the city's historical significance.

Financial and Business Hub

Today, Frankfurt holds the distinction of being one of the world's most important financial centers. It's home to the European Central Bank, the German Stock Exchange, and numerous multinational corporations. The towering skyscrapers that dominate the skyline house banks, financial institutions, and international companies, underscoring the city's role as a global economic powerhouse.

Cultural Diversity

Frankfurt's diverse population contributes to its vibrant cultural scene. The city is a melting pot of cultures, resulting in a dynamic mix of traditions, languages, and cuisines. This diversity is showcased in the various neighborhoods, each with its own distinct character and atmosphere.

Arts and Culture

The city's commitment to the arts is evident in its plethora of museums, galleries, and cultural institutions. The Museum Embankment, lined with world-class museums, is a cultural haven for art enthusiasts. From classical art to contemporary exhibitions, Frankfurt's cultural landscape offers a rich and diverse array of artistic experiences.

Green Spaces and Modern Infrastructure

Despite its status as a bustling financial center, Frankfurt values its green spaces. The River Main's picturesque promenades, expansive parks, and botanical gardens provide an oasis of relaxation amid the urban hustle. The city's efficient public transportation system, including an extensive network of trams, buses, and trains, ensures that exploring Frankfurt's offerings is both convenient and sustainable.

Gateway to Europe

Given its central location in Europe, Frankfurt serves as a major transportation hub. Frankfurt Airport, one of the busiest in the world, connects the city to a multitude of international destinations. This accessibility makes Frankfurt an ideal starting point for exploring not only Germany but also the rest of Europe.

Brief History of Frankfurt

Frankfurt's history is a tapestry woven with threads of conquest, trade, culture, and resilience. From its humble beginnings as a Roman settlement to its present-day status as a global financial hub, the city's journey through time is a fascinating narrative of growth and transformation.

Roman Origins and Early Settlement

The origins of Frankfurt can be traced back to ancient Roman times when a settlement called "Nida" was established along the River Main. This outpost served as a crucial crossing point on the Roman road network and played a role in trade and military operations. Over the centuries, the settlement evolved and expanded into the city we know today.

Medieval Importance and Imperial Coronations

During the Middle Ages, Frankfurt gained prominence as a free imperial city within the Holy Roman Empire. Its strategic location at the intersection of major trade routes contributed to its economic prosperity. The city hosted numerous imperial coronation ceremonies in the impressive St. Bartholomew's Cathedral, solidifying its status as a center of power and influence.

Rise of Trade and Commerce
Frankfurt's mercantile history continued to flourish, with the establishment of trade fairs that attracted merchants from all corners of Europe. The Frankfurt Trade Fair, dating back to the 12th century, became a key event for economic exchange, cultural interaction, and the introduction of novel goods and ideas.

Enlightenment and Cultural Significance
The city also played a significant role in the intellectual and cultural realms. The birthplace of Johann Wolfgang von Goethe, one of Germany's most celebrated writers, Frankfurt became a hub of literary and artistic creativity during the Enlightenment period. The legacy of Goethe and other influential figures is preserved in museums and cultural institutions across the city.

Modern Challenges and Resilience
Frankfurt faced numerous challenges in its history, including the devastation of the Thirty Years' War and the destruction caused by World War II. The city's rebuilding efforts after the war were nothing short of remarkable, as it transformed from ruins to a thriving metropolis within a few decades. This spirit of resilience

and determination is deeply ingrained in Frankfurt's identity.

Financial Center of Europe
In the latter half of the 20th century, Frankfurt emerged as a financial powerhouse. The establishment of the European Central Bank and the presence of major financial institutions solidified the city's reputation as one of the world's leading financial centers. The striking skyscrapers that dominate the skyline are a testament to Frankfurt's modern economic significance.

Cultural Significance of Frankfurt

Frankfurt's cultural tapestry is a blend of traditions, artistic expressions, and intellectual pursuits that have shaped the city's identity and enriched its global standing. As a hub of history, innovation, and creativity,

Frankfurt's cultural significance resonates through its architecture, institutions, festivals, and the diverse communities that call the city home.

Literary and Artistic Heritage

The city's literary legacy is exemplified by the towering presence of Johann Wolfgang von Goethe, whose birthplace stands as a testament to his enduring impact on German literature. The Goethe House and Museum offer a glimpse into his life and work, preserving the spirit of the Romantic era. Alongside Goethe, Frankfurt nurtured the talents of writers like Friedrich Schiller and the Brothers Grimm, whose fairy tales have captivated generations.

Museums and Galleries

Frankfurt boasts an impressive array of museums and galleries that span art, history, science, and culture. The Museum Embankment, located along the River Main, is a collection of world-class museums that include the Städel Museum, showcasing European art from the Middle Ages to contemporary works, and the Senckenberg Natural History Museum, which offers a journey through Earth's history. These institutions not only enrich the local cultural landscape but also attract international attention.

Theater and Performing Arts

The city's commitment to the performing arts is reflected in its numerous theaters and venues. The Frankfurt Opera House, renowned for its exceptional productions, is a focal point for opera and ballet enthusiasts. The Schauspiel Frankfurt offers a diverse range of plays and performances, celebrating both classic and contemporary theater. The English Theatre Frankfurt, Europe's largest English-language theater, further contributes to the city's cultural vibrancy.

Festivals and Events

Frankfurt's calendar is adorned with vibrant festivals that celebrate art, music, literature, and more. The Museum Embankment Festival draws crowds with live music, culinary delights, and artistic exhibitions. The Frankfurt Book Fair, one of the world's largest, brings publishers, authors, and book lovers together to explore the written word. During Christmas, the city's markets transform into a magical wonderland, offering festive cheer and traditional crafts.

Diverse Communities

Frankfurt's cultural significance is amplified by its diverse population. The city is a melting pot of cultures, languages, and traditions, creating a dynamic environment where global perspectives converge. This diversity is evident in the neighborhoods, where international influences contribute to culinary offerings, local celebrations, and a rich tapestry of human stories.

Architectural Marvels
Frankfurt's architecture echoes its historical journey. The Romer Square, with its picturesque half-timbered houses, transports visitors back to medieval times. The juxtaposition of these historic structures against the modern skyscrapers in the financial district symbolizes the city's evolution from its imperial past to its current position as a symbol of progress and innovation.

Best Time to Visit Frankfurt

The optimal time to visit Frankfurt depends on your preferences, interests, and the type of experience you seek. Each season in this vibrant German city offers unique attractions, weather conditions, and cultural events. Consider these factors to decide when to plan your visit:

Spring (March to May):
Spring in Frankfurt brings a burst of color and rejuvenation as flowers bloom and outdoor spaces come to life. The weather gradually warms up, making it pleasant for exploring the city's parks, gardens, and outdoor attractions. The Palmengarten Botanical Garden is especially enchanting during this time. Additionally,

spring is ideal for cultural enthusiasts, with various festivals, art exhibitions, and events taking place.

Summer (June to August):
Summer is the peak tourist season in Frankfurt, thanks to the warm and sunny weather. The city's outdoor cafes, riverside promenades, and green spaces buzz with activity. The Main River becomes a hub for boat cruises and leisurely picnics. While the streets are livelier and there are numerous festivals and outdoor events, accommodation prices may be higher, and popular attractions can be crowded.

Autumn (September to November):
Autumn is a delightful time to visit Frankfurt, as the weather remains comfortable, and the cityscape transforms into a palette of warm hues. The fall foliage adds charm to the streets, parks, and surrounding countryside. It's an excellent time for exploring the Taunus Mountains or taking scenic drives on routes like the Romantic Road. Cultural events, including wine and harvest festivals, add a touch of local flavor to your visit.

Winter (December to February):
Winter in Frankfurt brings a festive atmosphere, with the city's Christmas markets stealing the spotlight. The Romer Square is adorned with twinkling lights and stalls selling crafts, mulled wine, and seasonal treats. The winter months are also a great time to explore the city's indoor attractions, such as museums, galleries, and

theaters. While temperatures can be chilly, the magical ambiance of the holiday season is truly enchanting.

Shoulder Seasons:
The transitional periods between seasons—spring and fall—can offer a balanced experience with fewer crowds and moderate weather. During these shoulder seasons (April-May and September-October), you can enjoy pleasant temperatures, manageable tourist numbers, and a blend of indoor and outdoor activities.

How to get There

By Air: Frankfurt Airport
Frankfurt Airport, officially known as Frankfurt am Main Airport, stands as one of the world's most prominent aviation hubs and a gateway to Europe. Situated just a few miles from the city center, this bustling international airport is a testament to modern

travel infrastructure and connectivity. Its sprawling terminals, efficient services, and global reach make it a key player in shaping Frankfurt's identity as a cosmopolitan metropolis.

Global Connectivity

Frankfurt Airport's strategic location at the heart of Europe positions it as a crucial connecting point for travelers from around the world. Serving as a hub for numerous international airlines, the airport offers an extensive network of flights to destinations spanning every continent. This connectivity not only facilitates travel to and from Frankfurt but also transforms the city into a crossroads of cultures, languages, and experiences.

State-of-the-Art Terminals

The airport is comprised of two main terminals, Terminal 1 and Terminal 2, each equipped with state-of-the-art facilities and services designed to cater to the needs of travelers. These terminals host a range of amenities, from duty-free shopping and diverse dining options to lounges for relaxation and business services. The terminals' efficient design ensures smooth passenger flow, even during peak travel seasons.

Airlines and Alliances

Frankfurt Airport serves as a hub for Lufthansa, one of Germany's flagship airlines, and is a member of the Star Alliance, a global network of airlines. Beyond Lufthansa, the airport hosts a multitude of other airlines, providing a diverse array of travel options and connecting routes. This blend of airlines and alliances enhances the airport's ability to accommodate different travel preferences and destinations.

Traveler Experience

Travelers passing through Frankfurt Airport are offered a seamless and modern experience. From efficient baggage handling and security procedures to multilingual staff and signage, the airport prioritizes passenger comfort and convenience. Travelers can also find a variety of services, including currency exchange, rental car agencies, medical facilities, and information centers to assist with their journey.

Environmental Initiatives

Recognizing its responsibility toward sustainability, Frankfurt Airport has implemented various initiatives to reduce its environmental impact. From energy-efficient infrastructure to waste reduction programs, the airport aims to balance its role as a travel hub with its commitment to environmental stewardship.

Accessibility to the City

The airport's proximity to the city center ensures swift access for arriving passengers. Efficient transportation options, including trains, buses, and taxis, make it convenient to reach downtown Frankfurt and explore its offerings. The well-connected transportation network extends the airport's influence beyond its physical confines, allowing visitors to easily immerse themselves in the city's culture, history, and attractions.

By Train: Main Train Stations in Frankfurt

Frankfurt's well-connected railway network and its strategically located train stations play a pivotal role in the city's accessibility, both within Germany and across Europe. The city's main train stations serve as bustling hubs of activity, offering seamless connections, modern amenities, and a glimpse into the vibrant rhythm of urban life.

Frankfurt Hauptbahnhof (Main Train Station)

Frankfurt Hauptbahnhof, often referred to simply as "Hauptbahnhof," stands as a central pillar of the city's transportation infrastructure. This historic railway station, dating back to the late 19th century, is not only one of Germany's busiest train stations but also one of its architectural landmarks. The station's grand facade and intricate detailing pay homage to its storied past.

Gateway to Europe
Hauptbahnhof's significance transcends its historical charm. As one of Europe's major railway intersections, it serves as a crucial gateway to the rest of the continent. The station connects Frankfurt to major cities across Germany and neighboring countries like France, Switzerland, the Netherlands, and more. The availability of high-speed trains, such as the ICE (Intercity Express), further enhances its accessibility and efficiency.

Facilities and Services
Hauptbahnhof's interior mirrors its external grandeur. The station's sprawling concourse is a bustling hive of activity, with travelers rushing to and from their platforms. A plethora of shops, eateries, and convenience stores line the concourse, catering to the needs of passengers. Travelers can grab a quick snack, shop for essentials, or relax in one of the cafes before their journey.

Connectivity to the City

The station's strategic location at the heart of Frankfurt ensures convenient connectivity to the city's public transportation network. Trams, buses, and the U-Bahn (subway) can all be accessed from the Hauptbahnhof, making it easy for travelers to reach their accommodations, explore attractions, and navigate the city.

Frankfurt Flughafen Fernbahnhof (Airport Long-Distance Train Station)

Situated directly beneath Frankfurt Airport, the Flughafen Fernbahnhof serves as a crucial connection point for travelers flying into or out of the city. This station is dedicated to long-distance trains, making it a vital link between air travel and train travel. The high-speed ICE trains connect the airport to major cities in Germany and beyond, facilitating seamless transitions between different modes of transportation.

Modern Amenities

The Flughafen Fernbahnhof is designed with the modern traveler in mind. The station's facilities include ticket counters, waiting lounges, luggage storage, and easy access to the airport terminals. Passengers can effortlessly move between the train station and the airport, streamlining their journey and minimizing travel stress.

Efficiency and Convenience

Both Hauptbahnhof and Flughafen Fernbahnhof exemplify Germany's reputation for punctuality and efficiency in public transportation. The precision of train schedules, clear signage, and multilingual assistance ensure that travelers have a smooth and enjoyable experience, even if they are navigating a new city for the first time.

By Car: Highways and Routes in Frankfurt

Navigating Frankfurt by car offers travelers the freedom to explore the city and its surrounding areas at their own pace. The city's well-developed road network, efficient highways, and scenic routes make driving an appealing option for those seeking to discover both urban and rural treasures. Here's a closer look at the highways and routes that facilitate easy travel by car in and around Frankfurt.

Autobahns and Highways

Germany's renowned Autobahn network extends its reach to Frankfurt, providing a swift and efficient way to traverse the region. The city is strategically connected to major highways that link it to other parts of the country and neighboring countries. The A3, A5, and A66 are among the primary Autobahns that intersect or pass through Frankfurt, offering connections to cities like Cologne, Munich, and Basel.

Efficiency and Speed

The Autobahn system is known for its well-maintained roadways and lack of speed limits on certain sections. While some portions have recommended speed limits, other segments allow for drivers to experience the thrill of high-speed travel. However, it's important to adhere to safety regulations and exercise caution, especially when sharing the road with other vehicles.

Scenic Routes

For those who prefer a more leisurely and scenic journey, Frankfurt and its environs offer a plethora of picturesque routes. The Romantic Road, a famous tourist route, passes through nearby towns and villages, allowing travelers to experience the charm of traditional

German architecture, rolling countryside, and historical landmarks.

Parking and Accessibility
Parking options in Frankfurt range from street-side spots to secure parking garages. While the city center can be bustling, especially during business hours, ample parking facilities are available near major attractions, shopping districts, and transit points. Many hotels also offer parking options for guests.

Exploring Beyond the City
Frankfurt's strategic location in central Germany makes it an ideal starting point for day trips and longer excursions. The nearby Taunus Mountains offer scenic drives and hiking opportunities, while charming towns like Heidelberg and Würzburg are easily reachable by car. The flexibility of driving allows travelers to explore beyond city limits and uncover hidden gems in the surrounding regions.

Navigation and Tools
Modern navigation systems, GPS devices, and smartphone apps can greatly aid travelers in navigating Frankfurt's roads. They provide real-time traffic updates, alternative routes, and points of interest along the way.

CHAPTER 2: TIPS AND CONSIDERATION

Visiting Frankfurt on a Budget

Frankfurt, often associated with its status as a financial hub, might seem like an expensive destination at first glance. However, with smart planning and a bit of savvy, exploring this vibrant city on a budget is entirely feasible. From affordable accommodations to free and low-cost attractions, here's how to make the most of your Frankfurt experience without breaking the bank.

1. Accommodation: Start by looking for budget-friendly lodging options. Hostels, guesthouses, and budget hotels can provide comfortable stays without straining your wallet. Booking in advance and considering accommodations slightly outside the city center can also yield cost-effective options.

2. Free and Low-Cost Attractions: Frankfurt offers a range of attractions that won't dent your budget. Wander through the charming Romer Square, soak in the city's architectural marvels, and take a leisurely stroll along the River Main's promenade. Many museums and galleries offer free admission on specific days or during certain hours, so plan your visits accordingly.

3. City Card: Consider purchasing the Frankfurt Card, which offers discounts on public transportation, museum entrances, and tours. This card can be a cost-effective way to explore the city's offerings while saving on individual admission fees.

4. Picnics and Street Food: Instead of dining at pricey restaurants, opt for picnics in the city's parks or by the riverbanks. Grab some fresh produce from local markets or enjoy affordable street food from stalls and food trucks. Don't miss trying the local specialty, the savory "Handkase mit Musik."

5. Public Transportation: Frankfurt boasts an efficient and well-connected public transportation system. Purchase a day pass or a multi-day ticket for unlimited rides on trams, buses, and trains. This allows you to move around the city without worrying about individual fares.

6. Markets and Flea Markets: Explore the city's markets for a budget-friendly shopping experience. From the Kleinmarkthalle, where you can savor local delicacies, to the various flea markets that offer unique finds, these spots provide a glimpse into local life without straining your budget.

7. Outdoor Exploration: Frankfurt's green spaces are open to all. Spend time in parks like the Palmengarten or the Nizza Park, which offer tranquil settings for relaxation, picnics, and even sunbathing during the warmer months.

8. Walking Tours: Many tour companies offer budget-friendly walking tours that provide insights into Frankfurt's history, culture, and landmarks. These tours often operate on a pay-what-you-wish basis, allowing you to contribute what you can afford.

Getting Around Frankfurt

Navigating Frankfurt is a breeze thanks to its efficient and well-connected transportation system. Whether you prefer public transport, walking, or cycling, the city offers a range of options that make exploring its diverse neighborhoods, cultural attractions, and vibrant streets a seamless experience.

Public Transportation:

Frankfurt's comprehensive public transportation network is a cornerstone of city life. The integrated system includes trams, buses, S-Bahn (suburban trains), and U-Bahn (subways), all operated by the Rhein-Main-Verkehrsverbund (RMV). The convenience of this network means you can effortlessly travel across the city and even venture to neighboring towns and cities using a single ticket.

Trams and Buses:
Trams and buses crisscross Frankfurt, connecting various districts and attractions. They're a great way to get a local perspective as you move through the city's

different neighborhoods. Timetables are reliable, and electronic displays at stops provide real-time information on arrival times.

S-Bahn and U-Bahn:
The S-Bahn and U-Bahn provide efficient links within the city and to the outskirts. The U-Bahn serves more central areas, while the S-Bahn extends to suburban regions. These trains are particularly useful for reaching attractions like the Frankfurt Zoo, Städel Museum, and the bustling Zeil shopping district.

Cycling:

Frankfurt's bicycle-friendly infrastructure encourages exploration on two wheels. Dedicated bike lanes, shared paths, and bike racks make cycling a convenient option. You can rent bicycles from various providers, and the city's flat terrain makes pedaling from one place to another enjoyable and eco-friendly.

Walking:
Exploring Frankfurt on foot is a rewarding way to uncover its hidden gems and architectural marvels. The city's compact layout means many attractions are within a pleasant walking distance from each other. Take a leisurely stroll along the River Main's promenade or explore the historic Romer Square, immersing yourself in the city's atmosphere.

Taxis and Ride-Sharing:
Taxis and ride-sharing services are readily available for those seeking a more direct mode of transport. Taxis can be found at designated taxi stands or hailed on the street. Ride-sharing apps provide an additional option for getting around, offering convenience and often competitive rates.

Navigational Tools:
Modern technology simplifies navigation in Frankfurt. Smartphone apps provide real-time public transportation information, helping you plan routes, check schedules, and receive updates. Maps, both digital and printed, are invaluable resources for exploring the city's layout and finding your way around.

Shopping in Frankfurt

here are 5 of the best places to shop in Frankfurt, with estimated expenses:

1. Goethestraße: This is the most famous shopping street in Frankfurt, and it's home to luxury brands like Gucci, Prada, and Louis Vuitton. You can expect to spend a lot of money here, but you'll also find some of the best quality clothes and accessories in the city. Estimated expenditure: €200-€500 per person.

2. Zeil: This is another popular shopping street in Frankfurt, and it's home to a wider range of stores than Goethestraße, including Zara, H&M, and Nike. You can find more affordable clothes and accessories here, but you'll still need to budget for a decent amount of money. Estimated expenditure: €100-€200 per person.

3. Flohmarkt am Osthafen: This flea market is held every Sunday morning, and it's a great place to find unique and affordable items. You can find everything from clothes and furniture to antiques and collectibles. Estimated expenditure: €50-€100 per person.

4. MyZeil: This shopping mall is home to over 160 stores, including Zara, H&M, and Sephora. It's a great place to find a variety of stores in one place, and it's also home to a number of restaurants and cafes. Estimated expenditure: €100-€200 per person.

5. Galeria Kaufhof: This department store is one of the largest in Frankfurt, and it has a wide range of departments, including clothing, homewares, and electronics. You can find a good variety of brands here, and prices are generally reasonable. Estimated expenditure: €50-€100 per person.

Luxury Hotel Options

1. The Ritz-Carlton, Frankfurt: This 5-star hotel is located in the heart of Frankfurt, and it offers stunning views of the city skyline. It has a Michelin-starred restaurant, a spa, and a rooftop pool. Estimated nightly rate: €500-€1,000 per night.

2. Hotel Adlon Kempinski Frankfurt: This 5-star hotel is also located in the heart of Frankfurt, and it's a popular choice for business travelers. It has a number of restaurants and bars, a spa, and a fitness center. Estimated nightly rate: €400-€800 per night.

3. Villa Kennedy Frankfurt: This 5-star hotel is located in the Westend district of Frankfurt, and it's a popular choice for couples and families. It has a swimming pool, a sauna, and a steam room. Estimated nightly rate: €300-€600 per night.

Budget-friendly Lodgings

1. Hostel One Frankfurt: This hostel is located in the heart of Frankfurt, and it's a great choice for budget travelers. It has dorm rooms and private rooms, and it also has a kitchen, a bar, and a game room. Estimated nightly rate: €20-€40 per night.

2. A&O Frankfurt Ostend: This hostel is located in the Ostend district of Frankfurt, and it's a great choice for budget travelers who want to be close to the airport. It has dorm rooms and private rooms, and it also has a kitchen, a bar, and a game room. Estimated nightly rate: €15-€30 per night.

3. B&B Hotel Frankfurt City-Ost: This hotel is located in the Ostend district of Frankfurt, and it's a great choice for budget travelers who want to be close to the airport. It has modern rooms with free Wi-Fi, and it also has a breakfast buffet. Estimated nightly rate: €50-€70 per night.

CHAPTER 3:TOP TOURIST ATTRACTIONS AND CULINARY DELIGHTS

Romer Square

Nestled at the heart of Frankfurt's bustling city center, Romer Square (Römerberg) stands as a testament to the city's rich history, architectural beauty, and enduring significance. This iconic square is a captivating blend of medieval and Renaissance structures that tell the story of Frankfurt's past and its place in the present.

Historical Significance:
Romer Square's history dates back to the 9th century when it served as a marketplace and civic center. The name "Römer" derives from the old German word for

"Roman," referring to the Romer building that has been a focal point of the square for centuries. Over time, Romer Square became the site of important events, ceremonies, and trade fairs, cementing its role as a central hub of civic life.

Distinctive Architecture:
The square's architecture is a captivating fusion of architectural styles spanning several centuries. The Romer building itself, with its distinctive stepped gables and intricate facade, dominates the square. This structure has served as Frankfurt's town hall for over six centuries and remains an enduring symbol of the city's resilience.

Surrounding the square are meticulously restored half-timbered houses that showcase the traditional architectural style of medieval Germany. These buildings, adorned with decorative facades and colorful motifs, create a charming and picturesque backdrop that transports visitors to a bygone era.

The Fountain of Justice:
At the center of Romer Square stands the Fountain of Justice (Gerechtigkeitsbrunnen), a sculptural masterpiece that encapsulates the values and aspirations of the city. The statue depicts the allegorical figure of Justice holding scales and a sword, symbolizing fairness and the rule of law. The fountain is not only a work of art but

also a symbol of Frankfurt's commitment to justice and democracy.

Cultural Gatherings:
Romer Square continues to be a hub of cultural activities and events. Throughout the year, the square hosts markets, festivals, and celebrations that draw both locals and tourists. The square comes alive during Christmas with the famous Frankfurt Christmas Market, where the air is filled with the scent of mulled wine, roasted chestnuts, and festive cheer.

Visiting Romer Square:
A visit to Romer Square is like stepping into a historical fairy tale. Stroll along its cobblestone streets, admire the intricate facades, and take in the ambiance of centuries of history. The square's central location makes it easily accessible, and it's within walking distance of many other attractions, shops, and eateries in the city center.

St. Bartholomew's Cathedral

Dominating the skyline of Frankfurt with its majestic spires and intricate Gothic design, St. Bartholomew's Cathedral (Frankfurter Dom) stands as a towering symbol of faith, history, and architectural brilliance. This iconic cathedral has witnessed centuries of change, turmoil, and renewal, making it a revered monument in the heart of the city.

Historical Significance:

St. Bartholomew's Cathedral has a history that spans over 1,000 years, tracing its roots back to the 7th century. Throughout its existence, the cathedral has undergone multiple reconstructions, renovations, and additions, reflecting the evolving architectural styles and the city's growth. It has witnessed coronations of emperors during the Holy Roman Empire, making it a site of historical and cultural significance.

Gothic Architecture:

The cathedral's most striking feature is its stunning Gothic architecture. The soaring spires, intricate stonework, and elaborate ornamentation showcase the masterful craftsmanship of the medieval builders. The interior boasts intricate stained glass windows, towering vaulted ceilings, and ornate chapels, creating an atmosphere of grandeur and spirituality.

The Domturm:
One of the most iconic elements of St. Bartholomew's Cathedral is its towering Domturm, or cathedral tower. Offering breathtaking panoramic views of Frankfurt, the Main River, and the surrounding landscape, ascending the Domturm is a highlight of any visit. The climb up its spiral staircase is a journey through time and history, rewarded with a stunning vista at the top.

The Imperial Cathedral:
Throughout its history, St. Bartholomew's Cathedral has been closely associated with the Holy Roman Empire. It was the site of imperial elections and coronations, making it an important center of political and religious authority. The cathedral's significance in the context of the empire further adds to its allure and historical importance.

Restoration and Preservation:
The cathedral has endured its share of challenges, including damage during World War II. However, meticulous restoration efforts have ensured its preservation for future generations to admire and appreciate. The blend of original features and careful

restoration work provides visitors with a glimpse into the cathedral's rich past.

Visiting St. Bartholomew's Cathedral:
Located in the heart of Frankfurt's old town, St. Bartholomew's Cathedral is easily accessible for visitors. Whether you're an architecture enthusiast, a history buff, or simply seeking a moment of contemplation, the cathedral welcomes all. Guided tours provide insights into its history, architecture, and the stories embedded within its walls.

Palmengarten Botanical Garden

Nestled in the heart of Frankfurt, the Palmengarten Botanical Garden stands as a serene and enchanting haven that celebrates the wonders of nature. With its meticulously curated landscapes, diverse plant collections, and educational offerings, this botanical gem offers visitors a captivating journey through different climates, ecosystems, and botanical wonders.

Botanical Diversity:
The Palmengarten boasts an impressive collection of plants from around the world, showcasing the incredible diversity of flora that thrives in various climates and regions. From lush tropical rainforests to arid desert landscapes, each section of the garden transports visitors to a different corner of the globe. Rare and exotic species coexist alongside familiar favorites, offering a comprehensive exploration of Earth's botanical tapestry.

Tropical Treasures:
One of the highlights of the Palmengarten is its stunning collection of tropical plants housed in massive greenhouses. The Tropicarium is a lush oasis with soaring palms, colorful orchids, and vibrant blooms that thrive in the humid, equatorial climates. Visitors can experience the sights, sounds, and scents of these tropical paradises without leaving Frankfurt.

Seasonal Beauty:
Throughout the year, the Palmengarten transforms with the changing seasons. Spring bursts forth with a riot of colorful blossoms, while summer sees the outdoor gardens teeming with vibrant displays. Fall paints the

landscape with rich autumnal hues, and even winter offers a touch of magic as some greenhouses transport visitors to warmer climates.

Educational and Recreational Hub:
The Palmengarten is not only a place of beauty but also a hub of education and recreation. The garden hosts guided tours, workshops, and lectures that offer insights into the world of plants, conservation efforts, and horticultural practices. It serves as a valuable resource for students, researchers, and anyone interested in botany and ecology.

Tranquil Escapes:
For visitors seeking a moment of tranquility, the Palmengarten provides ample opportunities to unwind and connect with nature. The serene Japanese Garden offers a Zen-inspired oasis, complete with tranquil ponds, carefully arranged stones, and contemplative paths. The aroma garden engages the senses with a delightful array of fragrant herbs and flowers.

Family-Friendly Attractions:
The Palmengarten is a wonderful destination for families. Children can explore the Children's Plant World, where they learn about plants and ecosystems through interactive exhibits and hands-on activities. Family-oriented events and workshops make learning

about botany and nature an enjoyable experience for all ages.

Visiting Palmengarten:
Located just a short distance from the city center, the Palmengarten is easily accessible. Visitors can wander through its themed gardens, enjoy the beauty of seasonal displays, and relish moments of serenity amid the urban bustle.

Goethe House and Museum

The Goethe House and Museum in Frankfurt stand as a cherished tribute to Johann Wolfgang von Goethe, one of Germany's most illustrious literary figures. This historic site offers visitors a glimpse into the life, work, and legacy of the renowned writer, allowing them to immerse themselves in the world that inspired his genius.

Birthplace of Genius:
The Goethe House is the place where Johann Wolfgang von Goethe was born on August 28, 1749. The house itself is a striking example of 18th-century bourgeois architecture, and stepping through its doors is like stepping back in time. The rooms are meticulously preserved, offering an authentic representation of the domestic life of the Goethe family during the 18th century.

Literary Inspiration:
Goethe, often hailed as the Shakespeare of German literature, penned some of his most celebrated works within the walls of the Goethe House. He wrote the first version of his coming-of-age novel "The Sorrows of Young Werther" in this very building. The house's rooms provide insights into Goethe's creative process, offering a connection to the moments that shaped his literary masterpieces.

Authentic Interiors:
The interior of the Goethe House is a time capsule of 18th-century living. From the elegant drawing rooms to the intimate family chambers, the meticulously preserved furnishings, decor, and personal artifacts offer

a vivid depiction of the lifestyle of the era. Visitors can almost hear the echoes of conversations that might have taken place among the Goethe family members and their esteemed guests.

Goethe Museum:
Adjacent to the Goethe House is the Goethe Museum, a treasure trove of art and artifacts associated with the writer's life. The museum houses an extensive collection of paintings, prints, manuscripts, and personal belongings that provide further context to Goethe's multifaceted personality, interests, and artistic pursuits.

Cultural Significance:
The Goethe House and Museum serve as a pilgrimage site for literature enthusiasts, scholars, and admirers of Goethe's work. The site's cultural significance extends beyond national borders, attracting visitors from around the world who seek to gain a deeper understanding of the man behind the words that shaped German literature and culture.

Educational Experiences:
The Goethe House and Museum offer a range of guided tours, exhibitions, and educational programs that cater to diverse interests and age groups. These experiences provide deeper insights into Goethe's life, his

contributions to literature, and the historical context in which he lived.

Visiting Goethe House and Museum:
A visit to the Goethe House and Museum is an invitation to step into the world of a literary giant. The sites are easily accessible, located within the heart of Frankfurt's historic district. As you explore the rooms, artifacts, and stories, you can feel the presence of Goethe's creative spirit, leaving you inspired by his legacy.

Senckenberg Natural History Museum

Nestled in the heart of Frankfurt, the Senckenberg Natural History Museum stands as a captivating realm where visitors can embark on a journey through time, space, and the incredible diversity of life on Earth. With its extensive collections, interactive exhibits, and dedication to scientific exploration, the museum offers an immersive experience that ignites curiosity and appreciation for the natural world.

A Hub of Discovery:
The Senckenberg Natural History Museum traces its origins back to the 19th century, and over the years, it has evolved into one of the most prominent and comprehensive natural history museums in the world. Its mission is to foster understanding and awareness of the

planet's biodiversity, evolution, and the intricate web of life that surrounds us.

Diverse Collections:

The museum's vast collections span a remarkable array of topics, from paleontology and mineralogy to zoology and botany. Visitors can marvel at fossilized remains of ancient creatures, explore intricately preserved insects, and observe meticulously crafted models of prehistoric landscapes. These collections offer a window into Earth's past and present, showcasing the remarkable adaptations and evolutionary processes that have shaped life on our planet.

Dinosaurs and Beyond:

One of the museum's highlights is its extensive collection of dinosaur fossils and reconstructions. The life-sized models of these magnificent creatures transport visitors back to the Mesozoic era, providing a glimpse into the habitats and ecosystems that existed millions of years ago. Walking among the towering skeletons evokes a sense of wonder and awe, igniting imaginations and sparking interest in paleontology.

Interactive Learning:

The Senckenberg Natural History Museum takes education to new heights with its interactive exhibits. Visitors can engage with touch screens, multimedia displays, and hands-on activities that allow them to delve into the intricacies of natural processes, biodiversity, and ecological relationships. These immersive experiences make learning both engaging and enjoyable for visitors of all ages.

Planetarium and Special Exhibitions:
In addition to its permanent exhibits, the museum features a state-of-the-art planetarium that offers captivating shows about astronomy, the cosmos, and the mysteries of the universe. The museum also hosts rotating special exhibitions that delve into specific topics, from climate change to ancient civilizations, offering fresh perspectives and insights into our world.

Conservation and Research:
The museum's commitment to conservation and research extends beyond its exhibits. Experts at Senckenberg are actively involved in scientific studies and conservation efforts, contributing to a deeper understanding of our planet's ecosystems and advocating for their protection.

Visiting the Museum:
Located near Frankfurt's city center, the Senckenberg Natural History Museum is easily accessible for visitors. Its informative exhibits, engaging displays, and interactive elements make it an ideal destination for

families, students, nature enthusiasts, and anyone seeking to explore the wonders of the natural world.

Top 10 Best Local Cuisines in Frankfurt

Exploring Frankfurt's culinary scene is a delightful journey that reveals a rich tapestry of flavors, traditions, and regional specialties. From hearty comfort food to delectable desserts, here are the top 10 best local cuisines you must savor during your visit to this vibrant German city.

1. Frankfurter Wurst: No visit to Frankfurt is complete without trying the iconic Frankfurter Wurst, or Frankfurt sausage. These slender, juicy sausages are traditionally served with mustard and fresh bread, making for a quintessential street food experience.

2. Ebbelwoi and Handkase: Ebbelwoi, the local apple wine, is a cherished beverage in Frankfurt. Enjoy it in traditional Bembel (cider pitcher) alongside Handkase mit Musik, a pungent cheese marinated in vinegar and onions.

3. Green Sauce (Grunes Sosse): This tangy, herby sauce made from a blend of seven fresh herbs is a Frankfurt specialty. It's typically served with boiled potatoes and hard-boiled eggs, creating a refreshing and unique dish.

4. Rippchen mit Kraut: Satisfy your cravings for hearty comfort food with Rippchen mit Kraut. This dish features tender pork ribs slow-cooked with sauerkraut, resulting in a savory and fulfilling meal.

5. Frankfurter Rindswurst: Another sausage variety to indulge in, Frankfurter Rindswurst is a beef sausage that offers a slightly different flavor profile compared to the classic pork-based version.

6. Bethmännchen: These almond and marzipan cookies are a beloved dessert in Frankfurt, especially during the holiday season. Their distinctive shape represents the four fingers of a nobleman from the city's history.

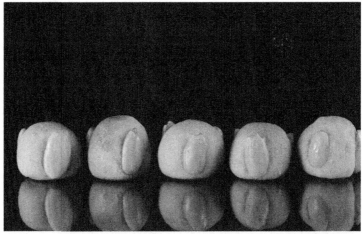

7. Frankfurter Kranz: A true treat for cake lovers, Frankfurter Kranz is a buttercream-filled sponge cake coated in caramelized nuts. Its circular shape and decadent taste make it a popular choice for special occasions.

8. Griesheim Handkase: This regional cheese specialty features a round, small Handkase topped with caraway seeds and served with onions, bread, and butter. It's a favorite among locals.

9. Kartoffelbrot: Potato bread is a staple in Frankfurt's cuisine. This hearty, dense bread is made with a mixture of rye and wheat flours, along with mashed potatoes, resulting in a unique texture and flavor.

10. Quetschekuche: Quetschekuche, a plum cake, showcases the delicious abundance of fresh plums in the region. The cake's buttery crust perfectly complements the sweet-tartness of the plums.

CHAPTER 4: NIGHTLIFE AND OUTDOOR ACTIVITIES

Bars and Pubs

Frankfurt's bars and pubs are more than just places to grab a drink; they are vibrant hubs of social interaction, culture, and relaxation. From historic taverns to modern cocktail lounges, the city's nightlife scene offers something for everyone, whether you're seeking a quiet evening, lively dancing, or a taste of local brews.

Historic Taverns:
Immerse yourself in Frankfurt's rich history by visiting its historic taverns. These charming establishments often boast centuries-old interiors, wooden beams, and rustic

ambiance. Here, you can enjoy traditional dishes, local wines, and ales while connecting with the city's past.

Ebbelwoi Bars:

Ebbelwoi, or apple wine, is a quintessential part of Frankfurt's culture. Ebbelwoi bars (Ebbelwoi Lokale) are the perfect places to experience this local beverage. These establishments offer a convivial atmosphere where locals and tourists alike gather to enjoy Ebbelwoi served in traditional Bembel pitchers.

Cocktail Lounges:

For those seeking a more contemporary experience, Frankfurt's cocktail lounges are a treat. Talented mixologists craft innovative and classic cocktails, allowing you to sip on concoctions that blend creativity with quality spirits. The stylish settings and carefully curated drink menus create an upscale atmosphere for a night out.

Live Music Venues:

Frankfurt's nightlife scene comes alive with the sounds of live music. From jazz and blues to rock and electronic beats, the city offers a variety of venues where you can groove to local and international bands. Whether you're a music enthusiast or simply want to dance the night away, these venues provide a dynamic experience.

Beer Gardens:

In warmer months, Frankfurt's beer gardens beckon with their outdoor charm. These spacious and communal spaces offer a laid-back environment to enjoy a cold beer, delicious food, and the company of friends. Beer gardens are a perfect way to bask in the city's pleasant weather while soaking up its social atmosphere.

Pub Crawls:

For a lively and diverse experience, consider joining a pub crawl. These guided tours take you through a selection of the city's best bars and pubs, allowing you to mingle with fellow travelers and locals. It's a great way to explore different neighborhoods and get a taste of Frankfurt's nightlife variety.

Late-Night Eateries:

After a night of socializing, you might find yourself craving a late-night snack. Frankfurt's late-night eateries and food stalls offer a range of options, from mouthwatering kebabs to indulgent street food that satisfies those post-party hunger pangs.

Nightclubs and Dance Venues

When the sun sets in Frankfurt, the city's vibrant nightlife takes center stage with its pulsating nightclubs and dance venues. From electronic beats to eclectic music genres, these energetic spaces offer an electrifying atmosphere for those seeking to dance, socialize, and immerse themselves in the rhythm of the night.

Electronic Dance Music (EDM) Scene:
Frankfurt's electronic dance music scene is renowned worldwide, drawing music enthusiasts and DJs from all corners of the globe. The city's clubs feature internationally acclaimed DJs who spin cutting-edge techno, trance, house, and electronic beats that keep dance floors alive until the early hours.

Eclectic Music Selection:
While EDM might dominate, Frankfurt's nightlife caters to a diverse crowd with a wide range of musical tastes. You can groove to anything from hip-hop and R&B to Latin beats, reggaeton, and even live bands performing rock or jazz. The city's venues offer something for

everyone, ensuring a night of fun and rhythm no matter your musical preference.

Stylish Venues:
Frankfurt's nightclubs and dance venues often boast stylish interiors, state-of-the-art sound systems, and immersive lighting displays that create an atmosphere of sensory stimulation. Many venues are designed to cater to both dance enthusiasts and those who simply want to revel in the ambiance while sipping on cocktails.

Late-Night Party Scene:
In Frankfurt, the party doesn't stop early. Nightclubs and dance venues are known for their late opening hours, often continuing well into the early morning. This allows you to dance the night away, embrace the night's energy, and experience the city's vibrant nightlife culture.

Diverse Crowd:
Frankfurt's nightlife scene attracts a diverse crowd, bringing together locals, expatriates, and international visitors. This melting pot of people creates a dynamic and inclusive atmosphere, fostering connections and making it easy to strike up conversations with fellow revelers.

Themed Parties and Events:

Many of Frankfurt's nightclubs and dance venues host themed parties and special events that add an extra layer of excitement to the nightlife experience. From costume parties to themed DJ nights, these events provide unique opportunities to dance, let loose, and create lasting memories.

VIP and Lounge Areas:
For those seeking a more upscale experience, many nightclubs offer VIP and lounge areas where you can enjoy bottle service, a more intimate setting, and a heightened level of service. These areas are perfect for celebrating special occasions or simply enjoying a more exclusive evening out.

Safety and Vibrant Atmosphere:
Frankfurt's nightlife scene is known for its safety and vibrant atmosphere. The city's well-regulated venues ensure that patrons can enjoy their night out with peace of mind. Whether you're exploring the popular clubs or the hidden gems, you'll find an energetic and welcoming environment.

Jazz and Live Music Bars

Frankfurt's jazz and live music bars offer a melodic escape for music enthusiasts and night owls alike. From sultry jazz notes to lively tunes spanning various genres, these venues create an intimate setting where you can immerse yourself in live performances, sip on your favorite drink, and revel in the magic of music.

Jazz Jams and Improvisation:
The city's jazz bars are known for hosting captivating live performances that showcase the improvisational prowess of talented musicians. These cozy spaces often feature jazz jams where artists collaborate and create unique musical experiences, infusing the night with spontaneity and creative energy.

Eclectic Music Lineup:
While jazz might be a highlight, Frankfurt's live music bars often curate a diverse lineup that caters to different musical tastes. You can find bars that host rock bands, acoustic duos, soulful singers, and even classical ensembles, ensuring that there's something for everyone to enjoy.

Intimate Settings:
One of the charms of jazz and live music bars is their intimate settings. These venues typically have a cozy ambiance, allowing you to get up close and personal with the performers. The smaller spaces create an immersive experience where you can feel the music reverberate through your soul.

Supporting Local Talent:
Frankfurt's jazz and live music bars play a crucial role in nurturing local talent. Emerging artists often find their start in these venues, honing their skills and captivating audiences with their passion and creativity. Supporting these musicians adds to the city's vibrant cultural scene.

Late-Night Music:
Many jazz and live music bars in Frankfurt keep their doors open late into the night. This makes them perfect destinations for a post-dinner outing or a nightcap after exploring the city's other attractions. The relaxed atmosphere encourages you to unwind and let the music carry you away.

Artistic Vibes:
Jazz and live music bars often have a distinct artistic vibe. The walls may be adorned with music memorabilia, vintage instruments, and colorful décor

that contribute to the overall atmosphere. The combination of music and visual aesthetics creates an immersive sensory experience.

Local and International Acts:
Frankfurt's live music scene attracts both local talents and international acts passing through the city. This diversity in performers ensures that you can enjoy a range of musical styles and influences, broadening your musical horizons.

Connecting with Music Lovers:
These venues bring together like-minded individuals who share a passion for music. Whether you're enjoying the tunes with friends, striking up conversations with fellow patrons, or simply appreciating the sounds in solitude, jazz and live music bars provide an avenue for connecting over shared musical experiences.

Parks and Green Spaces

Amidst the urban hustle and bustle of Frankfurt, a serene and rejuvenating world awaits in the city's parks and green spaces. From sprawling gardens to peaceful riverbanks, these natural havens provide a breath of fresh air, a place to unwind, and a connection to the beauty of the outdoors.

Palmengarten Botanical Garden:

The Palmengarten is a botanical wonderland that transports visitors across different climates and ecosystems. Its meticulously curated landscapes feature a stunning array of plants, from tropical rainforests to desert succulents. Meandering through themed gardens, visitors can soak up the tranquil atmosphere while marveling at the diversity of plant life.

Stadtwald (City Forest):

The Stadtwald, Frankfurt's expansive city forest, offers a rustic retreat for nature lovers. With its winding trails, serene ponds, and shaded pathways, it's a paradise for walkers, joggers, and cyclists. The forest's biodiversity, encompassing flora and fauna, creates an immersive experience that feels worlds away from the urban center.

Nizza Park:

Nestled along the banks of the River Main, Nizza Park provides a picturesque setting for relaxation. The park's manicured lawns, vibrant flower beds, and inviting benches make it an ideal spot for picnics, leisurely strolls, or simply gazing at the tranquil waters of the river.

Grüneburgpark:

Grüneburgpark offers a blend of open spaces and lush gardens. Its wide lawns invite families and friends to play sports or enjoy a sunny afternoon. The park's tranquil ponds, tree-lined pathways, and proximity to educational institutions make it a serene oasis for both leisure and learning.

Ostpark:

Ostpark is a true haven for those seeking active outdoor pursuits. With sports facilities, playgrounds, and even a lake for boating, the park caters to a variety of recreational interests. Its sprawling landscapes provide ample space for jogging, cycling, and enjoying the company of friends and family.

Mainufer (Riverbank):

The Main River's picturesque riverbank, known as Mainufer, is a beloved gathering place for locals and visitors alike. The tree-lined promenade offers stunning views of the city skyline, creating a perfect backdrop for leisurely walks, picnics, and serene moments by the water.

Stadtpark:
Stadtpark, located in the Sachsenhausen district, is a favorite spot for outdoor enthusiasts. This park features lush lawns, a large pond, and walking trails that wind through its natural beauty. The peaceful ambiance is perfect for relaxation and rejuvenation.

Günthersburgpark:
Günthersburgpark seamlessly blends recreational spaces with historical charm. The park's elegant gardens, ponds, and historic structures create a picturesque setting for leisurely strolls, reading, and enjoying the company of friends in a tranquil environment.

Connection to Nature:
Frankfurt's parks and green spaces offer more than just a break from city life; they provide an opportunity to reconnect with nature. Whether it's the rustling of leaves, the scent of flowers, or the soothing sound of flowing water, these spaces engage the senses and provide a sense of calm and grounding.

Community and Culture:

These green oases also play host to various cultural events, concerts, and festivals throughout the year. From open-air film screenings to music performances, they create a space where the community can come together, celebrate, and share moments of joy.

River Main Activities

The River Main flows through the heart of Frankfurt, adding a touch of serenity and a multitude of recreational opportunities to the bustling city. From leisurely cruises to vibrant festivals, the river provides a dynamic backdrop for a wide range of activities that allow residents and visitors alike to connect with its waterside allure.

Boat Cruises and Tours:

Exploring Frankfurt from the vantage point of the River Main is an enchanting experience. Boat cruises and tours offer panoramic views of the city's skyline, historic landmarks, and charming neighborhoods. Whether you're on a sightseeing cruise, a romantic dinner cruise, or a guided tour, the gentle sway of the boat and the glimmering reflections on the water create an unforgettable ambiance.

Canoeing and Kayaking:
For those seeking a more active water adventure, canoeing and kayaking along the River Main provide an opportunity to paddle through the heart of the city. Whether you're a novice or an experienced paddler, navigating the river's currents allows you to see Frankfurt's landmarks from a unique perspective.

Riverside Walks and Bike Rides:
The River Main is flanked by picturesque promenades and biking paths that invite pedestrians and cyclists to explore its banks. These paths are perfect for leisurely walks, energetic jogs, or leisurely bike rides, offering a scenic route to take in the city's sights and enjoy the calming presence of the water.

Mainuferfest:
The Mainuferfest is an annual festival that celebrates the River Main and its cultural significance. This vibrant

event brings together locals and visitors for days of live music, food stalls, art installations, and cultural performances along the riverbank. It's a lively celebration that showcases the river's role as a focal point of community life.

Picnics and Relaxation:
The riverbanks provide ideal spots for picnics and relaxation. Lay down a blanket, savor a homemade meal, and enjoy the serene ambiance as you watch boats pass by and the sun set over the water. It's a perfect way to unwind and savor moments of tranquility.

Fishing and Angling:
The River Main also offers fishing enthusiasts a chance to cast their lines and try their luck. Whether you're an experienced angler or a novice, the river's waters are home to a variety of fish species, providing an opportunity for a peaceful and fulfilling fishing experience.

Photography and Artistic Inspiration:
The River Main's picturesque views, juxtaposed against the city's architecture, create a captivating setting for photography and artistic endeavors. The changing light throughout the day casts different moods over the water, offering photographers and artists a canvas of natural beauty to capture.

Connecting with Nature and Community:
Engaging with the River Main's activities fosters a deeper connection to both nature and the community. Whether you're mingling with fellow passengers on a cruise, sharing a meal with friends by the river, or participating in a riverside event, the waterway brings people together and creates shared memories.

Day Trips to Surrounding Areas

While Frankfurt itself offers a wealth of attractions, the surrounding areas beckon with their own treasures waiting to be discovered. Embarking on day trips from Frankfurt allows you to explore charming towns, scenic landscapes, historical sites, and cultural gems that enrich your travel experience and offer a deeper understanding of the region's diverse offerings.

Heidelberg: A Romantic Escape:

Less than an hour away from Frankfurt, Heidelberg enchants with its romantic ambiance and historic charm. The iconic Heidelberg Castle stands majestically atop a hill, offering panoramic views of the town and the Neckar River. Stroll along the historic streets, visit the university, and immerse yourself in the poetic allure that has captivated generations.

Rhine Valley: Castles and Vineyards:

A journey along the Rhine River takes you through a fairytale landscape of medieval castles, charming villages, and lush vineyards. The Upper Middle Rhine Valley, a UNESCO World Heritage Site, offers boat cruises that reveal stunning vistas and the opportunity to explore towns like Rüdesheim and Bacharach.

Wiesbaden and Mainz: Historical Twin Cities:

Venture to the neighboring cities of Wiesbaden and Mainz, each with its own distinct character. Wiesbaden is known for its elegant architecture, luxurious spa culture, and vibrant cultural scene. Mainz, on the other hand, boasts a rich history, impressive cathedrals, and a lively atmosphere along the banks of the Rhine.

Taunus Mountains: Natural Beauty and Retreat:

Escape to the Taunus Mountains, a range of wooded hills and valleys that offer hiking trails, scenic viewpoints, and a refreshing break from the urban hustle. Explore quaint villages like Kronberg and Königstein, and relish the tranquility of nature's embrace.

Eltville and the Rheingau: Wine and Elegance:
Eltville, nestled in the Rheingau region, is a picturesque town known for its wine culture and charming architecture. Stroll through its historic center, visit vineyards, and indulge in wine tastings. The Rheingau's wine-growing tradition and beautiful landscapes provide an idyllic escape.

Bad Homburg: Spa Town Serenity:
Bad Homburg, with its healing mineral springs and well-manicured gardens, offers a retreat for relaxation and rejuvenation. The town's Kurpark, spa facilities, and the impressive Bad Homburg Castle create a tranquil atmosphere perfect for a day of unwinding.

Marburg: Medieval Marvel:
Marburg, a historic university town, boasts a fairy tale-like charm with its timber-framed houses, cobblestone streets, and Marburg Castle perched high above the town. Explore its medieval history, visit the university, and enjoy the vibrant student culture.

CHAPTER 5: EVENTS AND FESTIVALS

Frankfurt Book Fair

The Frankfurt Book Fair stands as an iconic event in the literary world, captivating book enthusiasts, publishers, authors, and industry professionals from around the globe. As the largest book fair in the world, it's not just a showcase of literature but also a cultural phenomenon that celebrates the written word, fosters creativity, and facilitates meaningful connections within the publishing industry.

Global Gathering of Literature:

Every year, Frankfurt transforms into a literary mecca as publishers, authors, agents, booksellers, and literary enthusiasts descend upon the city. The fair is a platform for publishers to present their latest releases, showcase upcoming titles, and explore potential collaborations on an international scale.

Rights and Licensing Hub:
The Frankfurt Book Fair is not only about showcasing books; it's a marketplace for the exchange of rights and licenses. Publishers and agents negotiate translation rights, film adaptations, and other licensing opportunities, making it a pivotal event for expanding the reach of literary works across languages and media.

Inspirational Author Talks:
The fair hosts a plethora of author talks, panel discussions, and presentations that delve into a wide range of topics, from literature and culture to industry trends and technological advancements. These sessions offer insights, spark conversations, and provide a platform for authors to engage with their readers and peers.

Spotlight on Diversity and Inclusion:
The Frankfurt Book Fair places a strong emphasis on inclusivity and diversity, showcasing voices from various cultures, backgrounds, and perspectives. Special programs and initiatives highlight literature from regions and languages that may not always receive international

attention, fostering a richer understanding of global literary landscapes.

Literary Awards and Recognitions:
The fair serves as a backdrop for the announcement of literary awards, adding an air of anticipation and celebration to the event. Awards for genres like fiction, non-fiction, children's literature, and more are presented, recognizing the exceptional contributions of authors and their works.

Networking and Professional Development:
Beyond its cultural significance, the Frankfurt Book Fair is a crucial networking hub for publishing professionals. It offers a unique opportunity to forge connections, establish partnerships, and stay updated on the latest industry trends, innovations, and best practices.

Public and Trade Days:
The fair is open to both the general public and trade professionals, allowing a wide audience to engage with books, authors, and the publishing industry. Public days create an accessible and inclusive atmosphere, while trade days cater to industry insiders seeking business opportunities.

Frankfurt Kids:

A special segment of the fair, Frankfurt Kids, focuses on children's and young adult literature. It's a vibrant space where publishers, authors, and educators come together to discuss the latest trends, share ideas, and promote literacy and learning among young readers.

Cultural Exchange and Dialogue:
The Frankfurt Book Fair fosters cultural exchange by welcoming guest countries or regions as the fair's spotlight, providing them with an opportunity to showcase their literature, art, and culture to a global audience. This dialogue fosters understanding and appreciation for diverse cultures.

Christmas Markets in Frankfurt

During the holiday season, Frankfurt transforms into a magical wonderland as its charming Christmas markets come to life. These enchanting markets, known as "Weihnachtsmärkte," are a beloved tradition that captures the spirit of Christmas, creating a warm and joyful atmosphere that resonates with locals and visitors alike.

Römerberg Christmas Market:
The heart of Frankfurt's Christmas magic is the Römerberg Christmas Market. Set against the backdrop of the historic Römer building, the market's stalls are adorned with twinkling lights, creating a fairytale scene. Traditional crafts, ornaments, and seasonal delights fill the market, inviting you to wander through a world of holiday enchantment.

St. Bartholomew's Christmas Market:
Nestled around the grand St. Bartholomew's Cathedral, this market exudes a medieval charm. Wooden huts sell handcrafted gifts, culinary delights, and festive treats. Carolers sing traditional songs, and the scent of roasted chestnuts and mulled wine fills the air, transporting you to a bygone era of yuletide celebrations.

Fairy Tale Christmas Market:
For a touch of whimsy, the Fairy Tale Christmas Market at the St. Paul's Church offers a unique experience. Inspired by Grimm Brothers' fairy tales, the market's stalls are adorned with characters and scenes from

beloved stories. It's a place where enchantment meets holiday cheer.

Mainkai Christmas Market:
Along the banks of the River Main, the Mainkai Christmas Market offers a picturesque setting for seasonal merriment. With its view of the illuminated skyline, this market invites you to sip on warm drinks, browse crafts, and relish in the beauty of the river by night.

Seasonal Delights:
Frankfurt's Christmas markets offer an array of seasonal treats that tantalize the taste buds. Indulge in traditional treats like "Bethmännchen" (almond and marzipan cookies), "Bratwurst" (sausages), and "Stollen" (fruitcake). Sip on "Glühwein" (mulled wine) or "Feuerzangenbowle" (mulled wine with a flaming sugar cube) to warm your spirits.

Handcrafted Treasures:
The markets are a treasure trove of handcrafted gifts, ornaments, and decorative items. From intricately designed ornaments to artisanal crafts, these markets offer the perfect opportunity to find unique and thoughtful gifts for loved ones.

Festive Entertainment:

Christmas markets are a hub of entertainment. Live performances, carolers, and musical ensembles create a festive ambiance that resonates with the joy of the season. The jovial spirit of the marketgoers, combined with the merry sounds, paints a scene of holiday delight.

Community and Tradition:
Frankfurt's Christmas markets are more than just places to shop; they are a celebration of community and tradition. The markets bring people together to celebrate the joy of the season, fostering a sense of togetherness that embodies the true spirit of Christmas.

Magical Atmosphere:
The combination of twinkling lights, rustic wooden stalls, and the festive energy of the crowd creates a magical atmosphere that immerses you in the holiday spirit. Walking through the markets, you'll find yourself transported to a world of wonder and enchantment.

Museum Embankment Festival

The Museum Embankment Festival in Frankfurt is an annual cultural celebration that weaves together art, music, dance, and culinary delights along the picturesque banks of the River Main. This vibrant festival transforms the city's riverside into a dynamic tapestry of creativity, offering a multi-day experience that draws in locals and visitors alike.

A Fusion of Arts and Culture:

The Museum Embankment Festival is a unique amalgamation of artistic expressions. It brings together museums, galleries, theaters, and cultural institutions to showcase their offerings to the public. Visitors can enjoy a diverse range of activities, exhibitions, and performances that span visual arts, literature, music, dance, theater, and more.

Open-Air Galleries and Exhibitions:

During the festival, the museum district's streets, squares, and riverfront promenades turn into open-air galleries. Art installations, sculptures, and interactive exhibits invite attendees to engage with art in a free-spirited and unconventional manner, blurring the lines between traditional gallery spaces and the outdoor landscape.

Live Performances and Concerts:
One of the highlights of the festival is its vibrant musical
and performing arts lineup. Stages are set up along the
riverbanks, featuring live music performances, dance
shows, theatrical acts, and street performances that span
genres and cultural backgrounds. From classical
melodies to contemporary beats, the festival's musical
spectrum resonates with diverse tastes.

Culinary Delights and International Cuisine:
The Museum Embankment Festival is a feast for the
senses, not only in terms of art and performance but also
through its culinary offerings. Food stalls and stands line
the festival grounds, offering a variety of cuisines that
reflect Frankfurt's international diversity. From local
specialties to global flavors, attendees can savor
delectable dishes while immersing themselves in the
festival's atmosphere.

Family-Friendly Activities:
The festival caters to visitors of all ages, with family-
friendly activities that engage children and adults alike.
Interactive workshops, hands-on art projects, storytelling
sessions, and puppet shows provide young festivalgoers
with a chance to explore their creativity and learn about
various art forms.

Cultural Exchange and Dialogue:
The Museum Embankment Festival goes beyond mere entertainment; it fosters cultural exchange and dialogue. With a program that often includes special themes or featured countries, the festival encourages attendees to explore diverse cultures, engage in discussions, and gain insights into global artistic perspectives.

Night of the Museums:
A highlight of the festival is the "Night of the Museums," where many of Frankfurt's museums remain open late into the night, offering a unique opportunity to explore their collections and exhibitions after hours. This nocturnal journey adds an air of mystery and excitement to the festival experience.

Sense of Unity and Community:
The festival brings together people from various walks of life, fostering a sense of unity and community. The shared experiences, joyful atmosphere, and collective appreciation of art and culture create connections that transcend individual backgrounds.

Wine and Apple Festivals

Frankfurt's wine and apple festivals are delightful celebrations that pay homage to the region's agricultural heritage, offering a blend of flavors, traditions, and cultural experiences that delight the senses. These festivals bring together locals and visitors to savor the rich harvests, indulge in culinary delights, and immerse themselves in the jovial atmosphere of these vibrant events.

Wine Festivals: A Toast to Viticulture:
Frankfurt's wine festivals celebrate the art of winemaking and the flavors of the region's vineyards. With the city's close proximity to renowned wine regions like the Rheingau, these festivals showcase an array of local wines, from crisp whites to robust reds. Wine enthusiasts and novices alike can sample varietals, learn about winemaking processes, and toast to the joys of good company and excellent wine.

Grapes and Gastronomy:
Wine festivals are an opportunity to pair fine wines with gourmet experiences. Local chefs and food vendors often collaborate to create dishes that complement the wines on offer. From regional cheeses and charcuterie to culinary delights inspired by international flavors, the festivals offer a diverse culinary journey that highlights the marriage of wine and gastronomy.

Live Music and Festive Atmosphere:
Wine festivals are known for their lively ambiance, with live music performances setting the tone for a joyous celebration. Musicians, bands, and performers take the

stage, creating an atmosphere where visitors can dance, socialize, and immerse themselves in the convivial spirit of the event.

Educational Workshops and Tastings:
For those interested in deepening their knowledge of wine, many festivals offer educational workshops and tastings led by sommeliers and wine experts. These sessions provide insights into wine appreciation, tasting techniques, and the nuances of different varietals, enhancing the overall festival experience.

Apple Festivals: A Harvest of Delights:
Frankfurt's apple festivals pay homage to the region's orchards and the abundance of apples harvested each year. These festivals celebrate the versatile fruit through a variety of activities, from apple-themed culinary creations to craft markets and family-friendly entertainment.

Cider and Culinary Offerings:
Apples take center stage during these festivals, with cider tastings, apple-based treats, and traditional dishes that showcase the fruit's versatility. From freshly pressed apple juice to delectable pastries, visitors can indulge in an array of apple-infused delights that highlight the fruit's sweet and tart profiles.

Family-Friendly Activities:
Apple festivals are often family-oriented, offering activities that engage children and adults alike. Apple picking, craft workshops, games, and live entertainment create an atmosphere of fun and togetherness, making these festivals perfect for a day of family bonding.

Cultural Insights and Traditions:
Wine and apple festivals provide a glimpse into the local culture and traditions of the region. Visitors can learn about the history of winemaking, the significance of apples in the local economy, and the role these fruits play in the culinary and cultural fabric of Frankfurt.

Community Connection:
Both wine and apple festivals foster a sense of community by bringing people together to celebrate the land's bounty and shared heritage. These festivals create a space where locals and visitors can mingle, connect, and create lasting memories over glasses of wine or bites of apple pie.

CHAPTER 6: RECOMMENDED ITINERARIES

1-2 Day Highlights

For travelers with limited time, Frankfurt offers a condensed yet captivating experience that highlights the city's rich history, vibrant culture, and iconic landmarks. In just 1-2 days, you can embark on a journey that immerses you in the essence of Frankfurt's charm and leaves you with lasting memories.

Day 1: Exploring the Essentials
Morning:
Begin your day with a visit to the Römerberg, the heart of Frankfurt's Old Town. Admire the historic Römer building and St. Bartholomew's Cathedral. Immerse

yourself in the medieval ambiance and snap photos of the charming half-timbered houses.

Late Morning:
Head to the Goethe House and Museum, where the renowned writer Johann Wolfgang von Goethe was born. Explore the museum's exhibits, which provide insights into Goethe's life, work, and the historical context of his era.

Lunch:
Indulge in local cuisine at a traditional German tavern or cozy café. Savor dishes like schnitzel, bratwurst, or hearty potato dishes while soaking up the local atmosphere.

Afternoon:
Stroll along the River Main's promenades for picturesque views of the city skyline. Cross the Eiserner Steg bridge to reach Sachsenhausen, known for its historic cider taverns. Enjoy a leisurely walk or rent a bike to explore the riverbank's beauty.

Evening:
For an authentic experience, dine at a traditional Apfelwein (apple wine) tavern in Sachsenhausen. Savor local specialties and raise a glass of cider to the Frankfurt spirit.

Day 2: Art, Culture, and Modernity
Morning:
Start your day at the Städel Museum, one of Germany's most important art museums. Explore its impressive collection of European art, from Old Masters to contemporary works.

Late Morning:
Take a leisurely stroll through Palmengarten, Frankfurt's botanical garden. Lose yourself amidst diverse plant species, themed gardens, and tranquil pathways.

Lunch:
Opt for a quick bite at one of the city's many street food markets or enjoy a casual meal at a café near the museum district.

Afternoon:
Visit the Main Tower for a panoramic view of Frankfurt's skyline. Ascend to the observation deck and marvel at the modern architecture harmonizing with historical landmarks.

Evening:
Conclude your trip with a visit to the Museum Embankment. If timing aligns, explore the cultural festival, exhibitions, or outdoor performances.

Wrap-Up:

In just 1-2 days, Frankfurt offers a well-rounded experience that captures the city's historical significance, cultural diversity, and modern dynamism. From exploring charming Old Town streets to indulging in local cuisine, immersing in artistic treasures to embracing riverside beauty, your short visit will leave you with a taste of Frankfurt's allure and a desire to return for more.

3-5 Day Exploration

With 3-5 days to spare, you have the opportunity to delve deeper into Frankfurt's diverse offerings, immersing yourself in its historical sites, cultural landmarks, surrounding areas, and hidden gems. This extended stay allows for a more comprehensive exploration of the city's rich tapestry.

Day 1: Historical Beginnings and Modern Marvels
Morning:
Start your exploration with a visit to the Römerberg, where you can delve into the history of Frankfurt's Old Town. Explore the Römer building, St. Bartholomew's Cathedral, and the Historical Museum. Immerse yourself in centuries of heritage.

Late Morning:
Discover the vibrant financial district by visiting the Eurotower and the skyscrapers that define Frankfurt's modern skyline. The Main Tower's observation deck offers panoramic views of the city.

Lunch:
Savor a leisurely meal at a café near the Römerberg, relishing the local flavors and historic atmosphere.

Afternoon:
Explore the Museum Embankment area, home to world-class museums. Choose from the Städel Museum, the Museum of Modern Art (MMK), the German Film Museum, and more. Delve into artistic treasures and cultural exhibits.

Evening:
Experience Sachsenhausen's lively atmosphere by dining in a traditional Apfelwein tavern. Enjoy hearty German fare and the conviviality of locals and visitors alike.

Day 2: Natural Beauty and Surrounding Wonders
Morning:
Embark on a day trip to the Rhine Valley, a UNESCO World Heritage Site known for its castles, vineyards, and charming villages. Cruise the Rhine River to admire stunning vistas and visit towns like Rüdesheim and Bacharach.

Late Afternoon:
Return to Frankfurt and explore the Kleinmarkthalle, a bustling indoor market. Sample gourmet treats, local produce, and international specialties.

Evening:
Dine at a riverside restaurant to bask in the glow of the illuminated skyline.

Day 3: Literary and Green Escapes

Morning:
Visit the Goethe House and Museum to delve into the life and works of Johann Wolfgang von Goethe. Gain insights into Frankfurt's literary legacy.

Late Morning:
Experience a change of scenery at the Palmengarten. Stroll through its diverse landscapes and themed gardens, immersing yourself in nature's beauty.

Lunch:
Opt for a leisurely picnic in one of Frankfurt's parks, savoring the tranquility and embracing the local lifestyle.

Afternoon:
Discover the Senckenberg Natural History Museum, home to an extensive collection of fossils, specimens, and exhibitions that showcase the wonders of the natural world.

Day 4: Day of Exploration and Relaxation
Morning:
Take a leisurely walk along the River Main's promenades. Visit the Städel Museum for a deeper exploration of its art collections.

Late Morning:
Visit the Main Tower for a different perspective of the city in daylight.

Lunch:

Savor an al fresco lunch at a café near the river, enjoying the peaceful ambiance.

Afternoon:
Explore Frankfurt's shopping districts, from luxury brands on Goethestrasse to boutiques in Zeil. Uncover unique finds and souvenirs.

Day 5: Cultural Insights and Farewell
Morning:
Visit the Jewish Museum Frankfurt to learn about the history and contributions of the Jewish community in the city.

Late Morning:
Stroll along the Main River and discover hidden corners or relax at one of the riverside cafes.

Lunch:
Indulge in a final meal of local cuisine, reflecting on the rich experiences of your visit.

Afternoon:
Spend your last moments wandering through the city's streets, soaking up the ambiance, and perhaps enjoying a final treat.

Week-long Immersion

A week-long stay in Frankfurt offers the opportunity for an in-depth and immersive experience, allowing you to truly connect with the city's multifaceted identity. From historical landmarks and cultural treasures to day trips and local experiences, this extended visit provides a comprehensive exploration of Frankfurt's rich heritage and vibrant present.

Day 1-2: Historical and Cultural Dive

Day 1:

Start your journey with a thorough exploration of the Römerberg and its surroundings. Dive into the Römer building, St. Bartholomew's Cathedral, and the Historical Museum to unravel Frankfurt's historical layers.

Day 2:

Delve deeper into the Museum Embankment's offerings. Spend the day exploring multiple museums, from classic art at the Städel Museum to contemporary pieces at the Museum of Modern Art (MMK).

Day 3-4: Urban Wonders and Day Trips
Day 3:
Discover the modern marvels of the financial district and take in the cityscape from the Main Tower's observation deck. Explore the bustling shopping districts, and treat yourself to culinary delights.

Day 4:
Embark on a day trip to Heidelberg. Immerse yourself in its romantic allure, exploring the iconic Heidelberg Castle and wandering through charming streets.

Day 5-6: Cultural Enrichment and Natural Beauty
Day 5:
Visit the Goethe House and Museum to deepen your understanding of the city's literary heritage. Then, take a relaxing stroll through Palmengarten to reconnect with nature.

Day 6:
Venture to Wiesbaden and Mainz, exploring their historical and cultural landmarks. Admire the

architecture, visit museums, and embrace the unique vibes of these twin cities.

Day 7-8: Surrounding Charms and Culinary Experiences
Day 7:
Experience the Rhine Valley's enchantment with a guided tour. Visit castles, enjoy scenic landscapes, and savor the charm of towns along the river.

Day 8:
Uncover the beauty of the Taunus Mountains. Hike scenic trails, explore quaint villages, and relish the peaceful retreat offered by nature.

Day 9-10: Immersion and Farewell

Day 9:
Revisit favorite spots, whether it's a museum, a café, or a picturesque street. Immerse yourself in the daily life of Frankfurt's residents.

Day 10:
End your journey with a visit to the Frankfurt Book Fair (if timing allows), celebrating literature and culture. Savor a farewell meal, reflecting on the incredible experiences you've gathered.

CHAPTER 7: PRACTICAL INFORMATION

Local Customs and Etiquette

As you explore the vibrant city of Frankfurt, it's important to familiarize yourself with the local customs and etiquette to ensure a respectful and enjoyable experience. Understanding the cultural nuances and social norms of Frankfurt will not only help you blend in seamlessly but also foster positive interactions with locals and create lasting memories.

Greetings and Politeness:
When meeting people, a firm handshake and maintaining eye contact are customary. Address people by their titles and surnames unless you are invited to use their first

names. "Bitte" (please) and "Danke" (thank you) are integral to interactions and are appreciated when showing politeness.

Punctuality:
Germans value punctuality and consider it a sign of respect. Whether you're meeting friends, attending an event, or visiting a museum, strive to arrive on time or a few minutes early.

Respect for Personal Space:
Germans value personal space and privacy. Maintain an appropriate physical distance when engaging in conversations, especially with people you don't know well. Avoid interrupting or raising your voice in public spaces.

Table Manners:
When dining out, wait to be seated rather than choosing your own table. Keep your hands on the table, not in your lap, while dining. It's customary to rest your wrists on the edge of the table. Indicate that you've finished eating by placing your knife and fork together on your plate with the prongs facing down.

Cash and Tipping:
While credit cards are widely accepted, it's a good idea to carry some cash, especially at smaller establishments.

When paying for services, it's customary to round up the bill and leave a small tip (around 5-10%).

Quiet Public Spaces:
Public spaces such as trains, buses, and waiting areas are generally kept quiet. Conversations should be conducted at a low volume, and speaking loudly on your phone or playing music without headphones may be considered impolite.

Recycling and Environmental Consciousness:
Germany places a strong emphasis on recycling and environmental sustainability. Be sure to separate your waste into appropriate bins and respect local efforts to reduce waste.

Dress Code:
Frankfurt is a cosmopolitan city with diverse fashion styles. However, when visiting more formal establishments or attending cultural events, it's advisable to dress neatly and avoid overly casual attire.

Cultural Sensitivity:
Be aware of cultural and historical sensitivities. When visiting churches or other religious sites, dress modestly. When discussing topics related to Germany's history, exercise sensitivity and avoid making light of serious matters.

Language:
While many locals speak English, it's appreciated when visitors make an effort to learn a few basic phrases in German. A simple "Guten Tag" (Good day) or "Bitte" (Please) can go a long way in establishing a positive rapport.

Useful Phrases for Navigating Frankfurt with Ease

While many residents in Frankfurt speak English, showing an effort to communicate in the local language can enhance your experience and interactions. Here are some useful German phrases that will help you navigate the city and connect with locals on a more personal level:

Greetings and Polite Expressions:
- Hello: Hallo / Guten Tag
- Good morning: Guten Morgen
- Good evening: Guten Abend
- Goodbye: Auf Wiedersehen
- Please: Bitte
- Thank you: Danke
- You're welcome: Bitte schön
- Excuse me: Entschuldigung
- I'm sorry: Es tut mir leid
- Yes: Ja

- No: Nein

Basic Conversational Phrases:
- How are you?: Wie geht es Ihnen? (formal) / Wie geht es dir? (informal)
- What's your name?: Wie heißt du? (informal) / Wie heißen Sie? (formal)
- My name is...: Ich heiße...
- I don't understand: Ich verstehe nicht
- Could you repeat that, please?: Könnten Sie das bitte wiederholen?
- Where is...?: Wo ist...?
- How much is this?: Wie viel kostet das?
- Can you help me?: Können Sie mir helfen?

Getting Around:
- Where is the train/bus station?: Wo ist der Bahnhof / die Bushaltestelle?
- How much is a ticket to...?: Wie viel kostet eine Fahrkarte nach...?
- Can you give me directions to...?: Können Sie mir den Weg zeigen zu...?

Dining and Food:
- A table for two, please: Einen Tisch für zwei, bitte.
- I'd like to order...: Ich möchte gerne... bestellen.
- The check, please: Die Rechnung, bitte.

- Water, please: Wasser, bitte.
- Can I have the menu?: Kann ich die Speisekarte haben?

Emergency Situations:
- Help!: Hilfe!
- I need a doctor: Ich brauche einen Arzt.
- Police: Polizei

Shopping:
- How much does this cost?: Wie viel kostet das?
- Can I try this on?: Kann ich das anprobieren?

Common Courtesies:
- Bless you (after sneezing): Gesundheit

Cultural Interactions:
- It's very nice: Es ist sehr schön.
- Your city is beautiful: Ihre Stadt ist wunderschön.
- I'm visiting from [your country]: Ich besuche aus [Ihrem Land].
- I'm here for [number of days]: Ich bin hier für [Anzahl der Tage].
- Your language is beautiful: Ihre Sprache ist wunderschön.

Emergency Contacts

While exploring Frankfurt, it's essential to be prepared for any unexpected situations that may arise. Familiarizing yourself with emergency contacts and services ensures your safety and peace of mind during your visit. Here are some important contacts to keep handy:

Emergency Services:

Police: 110
In case of any criminal activity, emergencies, or immediate threats, dial 110 to reach the police.

Medical Emergencies: 112
For medical emergencies, accidents, or urgent medical attention, dial 112 to reach emergency medical services.

Hospital / Ambulance: 112
In case of serious medical emergencies, including accidents or critical health issues, dial 112 for an ambulance to reach the nearest hospital.

Poison Control Center (Giftinformationszentrale): +49 69 19240
If you suspect poisoning or need assistance with medical advice regarding ingested substances, you can contact the Poison Control Center.

Consulates and Embassies:
Your Country's Embassy / Consulate: Check the contact details of your country's embassy or consulate in Frankfurt for assistance with passport issues, travel advisories, and emergencies.

General Safety Tips:

1. Stay Informed: Be aware of your surroundings and stay informed about the local news and any alerts or advisories.

2. Carry Identification: Always carry a form of identification, such as your passport, and keep a copy of your passport in a safe place.

3. Use Official Transportation: Stick to official taxis, rideshare services, and public transportation when moving around the city.

4. Secure Valuables: Keep your belongings secure and avoid displaying valuable items in public.

5. Stay Connected: Have a fully charged mobile phone and keep it with you at all times.

6. Know Your Location: Familiarize yourself with the location of your accommodation, nearby landmarks, and emergency exits.

7. Local Law Enforcement: If you need non-emergency assistance or have questions, you can approach local police officers for help.

8. Travel Insurance: Consider purchasing travel insurance that covers medical emergencies, trip cancellations, and other unforeseen circumstances.

Language Barrier:
In case of language barriers during emergencies, it's a good idea to have a translation app or phrasebook on hand. Many emergency services in Frankfurt have operators who speak English, but having essential phrases can be helpful.

Currency and Payment

Understanding the currency and payment options in Frankfurt is essential for a smooth and hassle-free experience during your visit. Here's a comprehensive guide to help you navigate financial transactions in the city:

Currency:

The official currency of Germany is the Euro (€), abbreviated as EUR. Euros come in both coins and banknotes of various denominations.

Cash and ATMs:

Cash is widely accepted in Frankfurt, and having some euros on hand is recommended, especially for smaller purchases, markets, and places that might not accept cards. ATMs, known as "Geldautomaten," are easily found throughout the city and offer the convenience of withdrawing cash in euros using your debit or credit card. Major credit and debit cards such as Visa, MasterCard, and Maestro are commonly accepted at ATMs.

Credit and Debit Cards:

Credit and debit cards are widely accepted at most hotels, restaurants, shops, and tourist attractions in Frankfurt. However, it's a good idea to carry some cash for transactions at smaller or local establishments.

Contactless Payments:

Contactless payments using cards or mobile devices (e.g., Apple Pay, Google Pay) are becoming increasingly popular in Frankfurt. Many retailers and restaurants offer this option for faster and more convenient transactions.

Tipping:

Tipping is customary in Frankfurt, and it's a way to show appreciation for good service. In restaurants, it's common to leave a tip of around 5-10% of the total bill. Tipping for services like taxis, hotel staff, and tour guides is also appreciated but not mandatory.

Value Added Tax (VAT):
Germany has a Value Added Tax (VAT) system known as "Mehrwertsteuer" (abbreviated as MwSt). This tax is included in the prices of goods and services. Visitors from non-EU countries can often claim a VAT refund for goods purchased and taken out of the European Union. Look for stores displaying the "Tax-Free Shopping" sign and inquire about the refund process.

Currency Exchange:
Currency exchange services are available at major airports, banks, exchange offices, and some hotels. While exchange rates may vary, it's advisable to compare rates and fees to get the best deal. Major banks and exchange offices are reliable options for currency exchange.

CONCLUSION

As you prepare to embark on your journey to Frankfurt, you're on the cusp of immersing yourself in a city that seamlessly blends its rich history with modern vibrancy. From the medieval charm of Römer Square to the innovative skyscrapers of the financial district, from the cultural treasures of the Museum Embankment to the tranquil beauty of its parks and riverbanks, Frankfurt promises a tapestry of experiences that will captivate your senses and enrich your understanding of this dynamic metropolis.

Navigating Frankfurt's diverse neighborhoods and cultural attractions is made easier with the insights gained from this travel guide. You'll wander through centuries-old streets, savor local cuisine that tells the story of the region, and embrace the warmth of the local customs and traditions. From the captivating stories of Goethe to the bustling energy of Christmas markets and cultural festivals, Frankfurt offers a kaleidoscope of experiences that resonate with every traveler.

As you explore the city's landmarks, engage with its people, and embrace its cultural nuances, you'll create cherished memories and connections that will stay with you long after your departure. Whether you're discovering historical landmarks, indulging in culinary delights, or simply strolling along the River Main, Frankfurt's unique blend of history, culture, and modernity will leave an indelible mark on your heart.

So, set forth with curiosity and an open heart, ready to uncover the hidden gems, embrace the local spirit, and experience the essence of Frankfurt in all its facets. As you traverse its streets, soak in its stories, and engage with its people, may your journey be a fulfilling and enriching adventure, and may the memories you create become a cherished part of your travel story. Safe travels and may your time in Frankfurt be truly unforgettable.

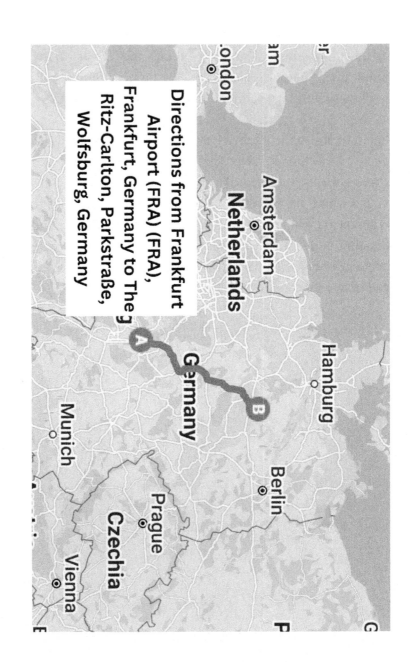

Directions from Frankfurt Airport (FRA) (FRA), Frankfurt, Germany to The Ritz-Carlton, Parkstraße, Wolfsburg, Germany

115

Directions from Frankfurt Airport (FRA) (FRA), Frankfurt, Germany to Villa Kennedy, Kennedyallee, Frankfurt am Main, Germany

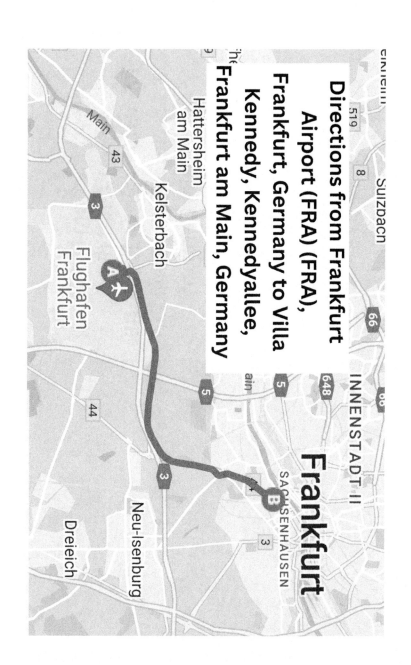

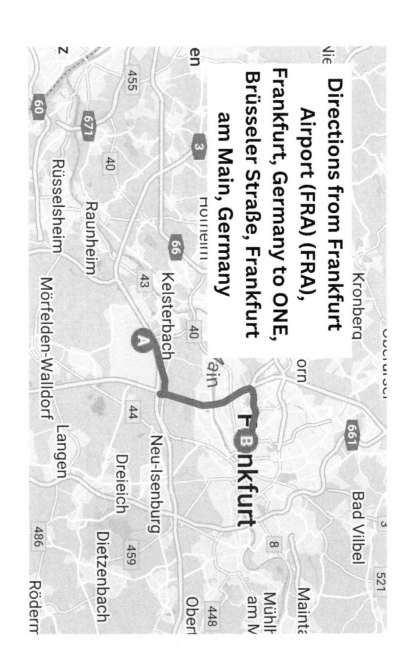

Directions from Frankfurt Airport (FRA) (FRA), Frankfurt, Germany to ONE, Brüsseler Straße, Frankfurt am Main, Germany

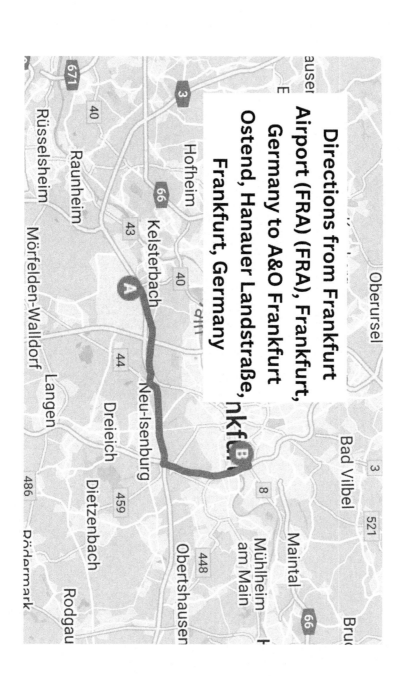

Directions from Frankfurt Airport (FRA) (FRA), Frankfurt, Germany to A&O Frankfurt Ostend, Hanauer Landstraße, Frankfurt, Germany

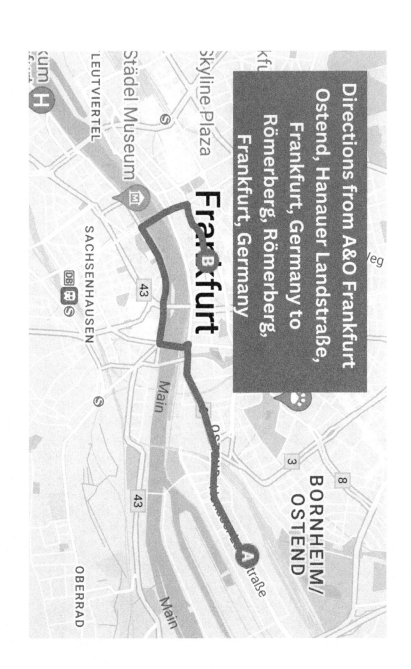

Directions from A&O Frankfurt Ostend, Hanauer Landstraße, Frankfurt, Frankfurt, Germany to Römerberg, Römerberg, Frankfurt, Germany

Directions from ONE, Brüsseler Straße, Frankfurt am Main, Germany to Palm Gardens, Siesmayerstraße, Frankfurt, Germany

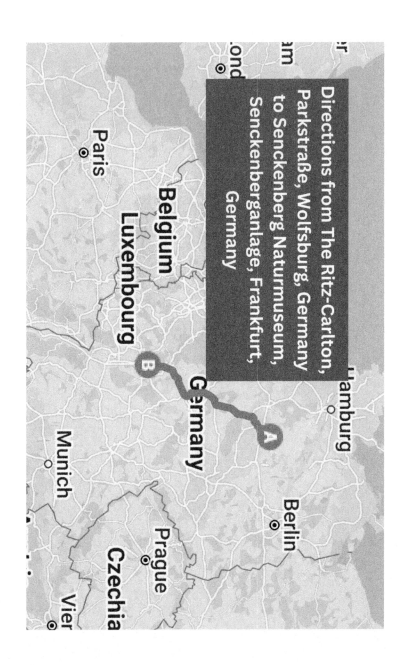

Directions from The Ritz-Carlton, Parkstraße, Wolfsburg, Germany to Senckenberg Naturmuseum, Senckenberganlage, Frankfurt, Germany

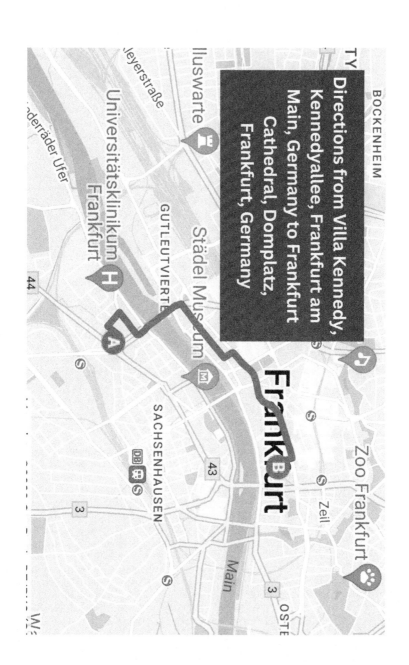

Directions from Villa Kennedy, Kennedyallee, Frankfurt am Main, Germany to Frankfurt Cathedral, Domplatz, Frankfurt, Germany

Printed in Great Britain
by Amazon

39326435R00069